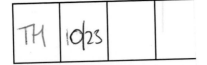

Oxfordshire Libr

D**an's Band**

'Jump In' and 'Dan's Band'
An original concept by Jenny Jinks
© Jenny Jinks 2023

Illustrated by Camilla Galindo

Published by MAVERICK ARTS PUBLISHING LTD
Studio 11, City Business Centre, 6 Brighton Road,
Horsham, West Sussex, RH13 5BB
© Maverick Arts Publishing Limited August 2023
+44 (0)1403 256941

A CIP catalogue record for this book is available at the British Library.

ISBN 978-1-84886-977-6

www.maverickbooks.co.uk

This book is rated as: Red Band (Guided Reading)
It follows the requirements for Phase 2/3 phonics.
Most words are decodable, and any non-decodable words are familiar,
supported by the context and/or represented in the artwork.

Jump In
and
Dan's Band

By **Jenny Jinks**

Illustrated by
Camilla Galindo

The Letter E

Trace the lower and upper case letter with a finger. Sound out the letter.

Across,
around

Down,
lift, cross,
lift, cross,
lift, cross

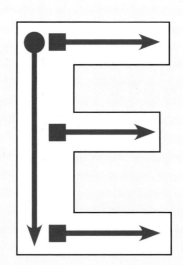

Some words to familiarise:

jacket   boots   puddle

High-frequency words:

it   is   you   me   puts   on

her   a   in   the

Tips for Reading 'Jump In'

- *Practise the words listed above before reading the story.*

- *If the reader struggles with any of the other words, ask them to look for sounds they know in the word. Encourage them to sound out the words and help them read the words if necessary.*

- *After reading the story, ask the reader what Dad jumped into at the end.*

Fun Activity

Draw a pair of boots that you would like to wear!

Jump In

It is wet.

Jen puts on her jacket and boots.

Splash!

Jen spots a big puddle.

Jump in!

Splash!

Dad spots a big, **big** puddle.

Stop!
That is not…

But Dad jumps in.

Dad is in the pond.
It is wet!

The Letter O

Trace the lower and upper case letter with a finger. Sound out the letter.

Around

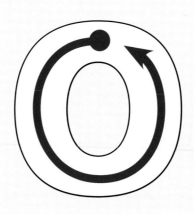

Around

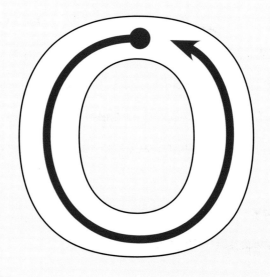

Some words to familiarise:

Dan   hammer   drill

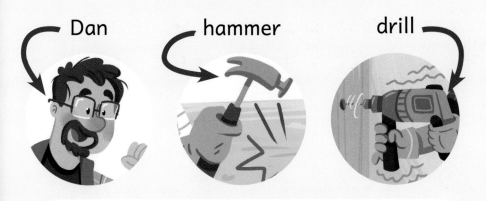

High-frequency words:

his   to   the   on

it   is   of   in

Tips for Reading 'Dan's Band'

- *Practise the words listed above before reading the story.*

- *If the reader struggles with any of the other words, ask them to look for sounds they know in the word. Encourage them to sound out the words and help them read the words if necessary.*

- *After reading the story, ask the reader what Dan likes to do.*

Fun Activity

Make up your own dance!

Dan's Band

Dan can jig and bop and tap.

Bop, bop, bop.

Max taps with his hammer.
Tap, tap, tap.

Dan bops to the beat.
Bop, bop, bop.

25

Cam gets his drill.
Buzz, buzz, buzz.

Dan bops to the beat.
Bop, bop, bop.

Dan gets on with his job.

But then the job ends...

Dan bops and pops and hops and taps.

It is lots of fun in Dan's band!

Book Bands for Guided Reading

The Institute of Education book banding system is a scale of colours that reflects the various levels of reading difficulty. The bands are assigned by taking into account the content, the language style, the layout and phonics. Word, phrase and sentence level work is also taken into consideration.

Maverick Early Readers are a bright, attractive range of books covering the pink to white bands. All of these books have been book banded for guided reading to the industry standard and edited by a leading educational consultant.

Pink
Red
Yellow
Blue
Green
Orange
Turquoise
Purple
Gold
White

To view the whole Maverick Readers scheme, visit our website at
www.maverickearlyreaders.com

Or scan the QR code above to view our scheme instantly!